# Motivating Superior Performance

5

# Motivating Superior Performance

Saul W. Gellerman

PRODUCTIVITY PRESS

Portland, Oregon

Volume 5 of the *Management Master Series*.
William F. Christopher, Editor-in-Chief
Copyright © 1994 by Productivity Press, Inc.

Productivity Press
P.O. Box 13390
Portland OR 97213-0390
United States of America
Telephone: 503-235-0600
Telefax: 503-235-0909

ISBN: 1-56327-063-3

Book design by William Stanton
Composition by Rohani Design
Printed and bound by Edwards Brothers in the United States of America

*Library of Congress Cataloging-in-Publication Data*

Gellerman, Saul W.
    Motivating superior performance / Saul W. Gellerman.
        p.    cm. -- (Management master series ; v. 5)
    Includes bibliographical references.
    ISBN 1-56327-063-3
    1. Employee motivation. I. Title. II. Series.
HF5549.5.M63G454    1994
    658.3'14--dc20                                    94-22594
                                                        CIP

APR 19 '96

BF

98 97 96 95 94    10 9 8 7 6 5 4 3 2 1

# —CONTENTS—

# PUBLISHER'S MESSAGE

The *Management Master Series* was designed to discover and disseminate to you the world's best concepts, principles, and current practices in excellent management. We present this information in a concise and easy-to-use format to provide you with the tools and techniques you need to stay abreast of this rapidly accelerating world of ideas.

World class competitiveness requires managers today to be thoroughly informed about how and what other internationally successful managers are doing. What works? What doesn't? and Why?

Management is often considered a "neglected art." It is not possible to know how to manage before you are made a manager. But once you become a manager you are expected to know how to manage and to do it well, right from the start.

One result of this neglect in management training has been managers who rely on control rather than creativity. Certainly, managers in this century have shown a distinct neglect of workers as creative human beings. The idea that employees are an organization's most valuable asset is still very new. How managers can inspire and direct the creativity and intelligence of everyone involved in the work of an organization has only begun to emerge.

Perhaps if we consider management as a "science" the task of learning how to manage well will be easier. A scientist begins with an hypothesis and then runs experiments to observe whether the hypothesis is correct. Scientists depend on detailed notes about the experiment—the timing, the ingredients, the amounts—and carefully record all results as they test new hypotheses. Certain things come to be known by this method; for instance, that water always consists of one part oxygen and two parts hydrogen.

We as managers must learn from our experience and from the experience of others. The scientific approach provides a model for learning. Science begins with vision and desired outcomes, and achieves its purpose through observation, experiment, and analysis of precisely recorded results. And then what is newly discovered is shared so that each person's research will build on the work of others.

Our organizations, however, rarely provide the time for learning or experimentation. As a manager, you need information from those who have already experimented and learned and recorded their results. You need it in brief, clear, and detailed form so that you can apply it immediately.

It is our purpose to help you confront the difficult task of managing in these turbulent times. As the shape of leadership changes, the *Management Master Series* will continue to bring you the best learning available to support your own increasing artistry in the evolving science of management.

We at Productivity Press are grateful to William F. Christopher and our staff of editors who have searched out those masters with the knowledge, experience, and ability to write concisely and completely on excellence in management practice. We wish also to thank the individual volume authors; Cheryl Rosen and Diane Asay, project managers; Julie Zinkus, manuscript editor; Karen Jones, managing editor; Lisa Hoberg, Mary Junewick, and Julie Hankin, editorial support; Bill Stanton, design and production management; Susan Swanson, production coordination; Rohani Design, composition.

Norman Bodek
Publisher

# INTRODUCTION

You've probably heard a lot about *motivation*. But what exactly is motivation, in a *practical* sense?

For a manager, motivation is making your people *want* to work as effectively as they can.

Motivation is important because it has a *multiplier* effect on how much work people do, and on how well they do it. Motivation doesn't merely improve performance; it *multiplies* performance (see Figure 1). Motivation can greatly increase the return on a company's investment in its people. This includes payroll, benefit programs, and the costs of recruiting, training, and insurance.

---

**MOTIVATION MULTIPLIES PERFORMANCE**

$$P = (K + S) \times M$$

P = Performance
K + S = Knowledge and Skills
M = Motivation

---

**Figure 1.**

Some of the effects of motivation are direct; others are indirect:

| **Direct Effects** | **Indirect Effects** |
|---|---|
| • job performance | • cost |
| • efficiency | • market share |
| • quality | • profits |

Can people be motivated quickly, easily, or cheaply? No.

Is it therefore, worth investing time, effort, and money to handle motivation effectively?

Absolutely. And note that the main cost is in *time* and *convenience*, not money.

# OUTLINE

This monograph sharply focuses on *eight* aspects of the complex, vital subject of motivation and the reasons why managers need to know about them. For more detailed information, please refer to the bibliography.

Section 1 looks at *individuals* because:

- Everyone has motives of their own that are a bit different from everyone else's.

- Everyone responds a bit differently to attempts by other people to motivate them.

- Finally, a few "motivational mistakes" are made so often that it's worth knowing how to avoid them.

Section 2 looks at *groups* because:

- Most work is done by groups rather than by individuals. So you must know how to motivate groups, as well as individuals.

- People act differently in groups than they do when they are alone.

- Groups can be strongly motivational themselves.

Section 3 reviews *leadership* for one obvious and two not-so-obvious reasons:

- The obvious reason is that leadership is the aspect of motivation that is most talked about, written about, and taken for granted.

The less obvious reasons:

- Most popular ideas about leadership are misleading because they're oversimplified.

- Despite decades of research, we still don't understand nearly as much as we need to about leadership.

Section 4 looks at *unions* because:

- A company that has a union will want to reduce the risk of shop-floor disputes and long, costly strikes.

- A company that does not have a union may be interested in keeping them out.

Interestingly, the strategy is the same in both cases.

Section 5 considers *money* for an obvious reason, but also for three not-so-obvious reasons:

- The obvious reason is that money, work, and management are all closely related. Nearly everyone gets most of their money by selling their work. And work, of course, is what most managers manage.

The not-so-obvious reasons for analyzing the effects of money on motivation:

- Money is seldom the most effective motivator.

- Money is, however, the most complicated motivator by far.

- Money is certainly the most expensive motivator. Therefore, to get the maximum effect from money, you have to know how to use it wisely.

Section 6 looks at *jobs* because:

- Jobs are usually designed for efficiency, not motivation. As a result, too many jobs are *boring*. Unfortunately, bored workers seldom do their work well.

- Smart managers win big gains in productivity by designing jobs to be varied and challenging.

Section 7 looks at *stress* because:

- Your motivational plans can go haywire when your people have to work under too much stress.

- On the other hand, too little stress usually means low motivation.

The eighth and final section is about *you:*

- How can you keep yourself motivated when everyone is making demands on you, and no one offers to help?

# 1

## INDIVIDUALS

It's time to refine our definition of motivation. Three tests determine whether someone is highly motivated. Such people have a goal or a purpose that is so important to them that in order to attain it, they're willing to:

- work harder

- take risks, and even

- accept some inconvenience or discomfort.

*A person who does not pass any of these tests is not highly motivated, no matter what he or she may say.*

### SOURCES OF MOTIVATION

Highly motivated people usually reach their goals more successfully than people who may be better trained, better equipped, or even smarter, but who are not as motivated as they are. For any individual, motivation has *two* sources.

### Internal Motivation

Some motivation comes from *within*. The individual has more-or-less permanent needs that are already built into his or her personality. These needs usually include various combinations of the following:

- survival needs, such as a secure income, and acceptance by others.

- comfort needs, such as being treated fairly and with respect and being liked.
- in some cases, winner's needs, such as achieving one's goals and being a leader.

## External Motivation

The second source of motivation is *outside* the individual, that is, in the environment. External motivation includes both opportunities and threats—anything that can affect the individual's chances of reaching his or her goals. These could include:

| **Opportunities** | **Threats** |
|---|---|
| • increased pay | • loss of job |
| • advancement | • unfair supervision |
| • more interesting work | • "dead end" jobs (no future) |
| • travel opportunities | • incompatible workmates |

*At any given time, the level of someone's motivation depends on whether, and how much, the external motivators either arouse or subdue his or her internal needs* (see Figure 2).

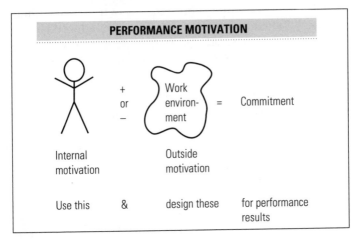

**Figure 2.**

# MYTHS ABOUT MOTIVATION

There are two ways to increase the number of highly motivated people in an organization:

- You can look for people whose needs are compatible with the organization's management style.
- You can adapt the organization's management style to the needs of the people who are available.

Most managers find the first method attractive because it *seems* to require less time and effort. Actually, it usually involves a lot of time and effort, and is *less* effective than the second approach in the long run.

When you get to know people really well, they nearly always turn out to have some features that you like, and others that you don't like. We are all, in other words, *imperfect*.

Your main responsibility as a manager is to make ordinary, imperfect people as *productive* as possible. If you keep that in mind, you'll avoid two of the most common mistakes about motivation. Both are based on *myths*.

**Myth 1:** If you can just find the right people for each job, they'll motivate themselves.

**The truth:** Some people are *self-motivated*. They work hard because they want to and need little or no external stimulation. Unfortunately, *very* few people are like this, and most of them are already in managerial jobs, or are self-employed. That's why it's unrealistic to spend a lot of time and money looking for people who don't need to be motivated.

Nevertheless, some companies are in a constant "hire and fire" cycle, hoping to find people who can work well *without* needing a lot of attention and encouragement. That strategy almost never works.

**Myth 2:** Everyone has a weakness that they can overcome if they really want to.

**The truth:** If you put people in jobs where their strengths really matter, their weaknesses won't matter (see Figure 3).

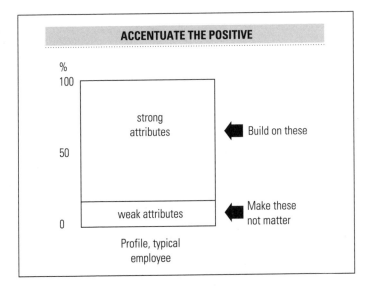

**Figure 3.**

Most so-called weaknesses are one or more of the following:

- a negative way to describe a strength (for example, someone who is extra-careful could also be criticized for being "fussy").

- a built-in feature that is unlikely to change (for example, someone who is outgoing will probably just continue chatting with other employees, even if told not to).

- a trait that is really "in the eye of the beholder." That is, we tend to be critical of people who are not like us.

The bottom line on weaknesses is that it seldom pays to try to change them. It is better to build on each individual's strengths than to be distracted by his or her so-called weaknesses.

# 2

# GROUPS

Employees tend to form *informal groups* amongst themselves that influence what their members do, and even what they think. In this sense, groups are powerful motivators. Unfortunately, however, groups often motivate their members to *resist management.*

## JOINERS AND LONERS

These groups affect some people more than others. *Joiners* are people who are influenced most by groups. *Loners* are people who are influenced least by groups. Of course, not everyone fits neatly into these two categories. Some people are joiners some of the time and loners at other times. The important point is that groups affect joiners and loners in very different ways.

### Why People Join Groups—Or Don't

The list below shows some reasons why different people might or might not join informal groups:

| Joiners | Loners |
|---|---|
| • feel helpless on their own | • feel able to care for themselves |
| • seek protection for themselves | • seek opportunity |
| • seek acceptance from others | • seek recognition for their achievements |
| • seek reassurance from others | • are confident they are right |
| • feel intense loyalty to a group | • can get along without group |

## Effects of Groups on Joiners and Loners

Here are some of the ways groups affect joiners and losers:

| **Joiners** | **Loners** |
|---|---|
| • support popular ideas they may not actually agree with. | • refuse to support popular ideas they don't agree with. |
| • defer to majority view. They often feel the majority must be right. | • are likely to hold out, and disagree with the majority. |
| • put unity, solidarity, comradeship above all other considerations. | • put their own interests above all other considerations. |
| • sacrifice opportunity for personal gain for the sake of the group. | • ignore group pressure to sacrifice opportunity for personal gain. |
| • deliberately limit their production if group demands it. | • resist group pressure to limit their production. |
| • may shun, snub, and disapprove of loners. | • may feel contempt for joiners. |

Loners tend to be promoted, or to leave the company altogether. That is why workplace groups, eventually, consist primarily of joiners. These groups often resist management pressure. They can be difficult to motivate, especially when unions are involved.

## REDUCING GROUP RESISTANCE

When informal groups have a negative attitude toward management, there are ways of reducing their resistance. The most important point is to make sure that you are not part of the problem yourself.

### AVOID CONFRONTATIONS

Don't create situations in which the group must back down on a matter of principle in order to please you. Members will almost certainly rally around that principle and probably won't believe any threats. *Never use a threat unless you seriously intend to carry it out. Empty threats destroy your credibility.*

### DON'T FLAUNT YOUR AUTHORITY

You do not need to show your employees that you are the boss. They know that perfectly well. The issue is to get these people to do their work properly. *If your employees resist you, it is probably because you have yet to prove that they can trust you not to abuse your authority.*

### FORGIVE OCCASIONAL MINOR INFRACTIONS

Showing good faith is not a sign of weakness. Workers won't take advantage of you unless you let them. Make sure, however, that employees know you expect to be repaid with extra cooperation when you need it. *Show that you're willing to meet your employees halfway if they reciprocate.*

### WORK WITH INFORMAL LEADERS

In most groups, a handful of assertive individuals usually stand out from the rest. Concentrate your efforts on them. If you can convince them that you are firm but fair, and that they can trust you to keep your word, they will convince the others. In fact, some informal leaders have become supervisors themselves. *Weak managers tend to regard leaders of informal work groups as trouble-makers. Strong managers regard them as potential allies.*

### DON'T MAKE YOUR EMPLOYEES' WORST FEARS COME TRUE

Most work groups expect bosses to be arbitrary, unfair, and threatening. All managers are handicapped by bad examples set by too many earlier managers. To get your job done properly, you need the cooperation of your employees. Prove through your actions that you don't fit that stereotype.

Show them that you can get your job done *without* abusing their dignity. *To win your employees' cooperation, treat them as allies, not enemies.*

Groups do most of the work in most organizations. If you can get a group to work with you, you'll probably win. But if a group works against you, you'll probably fail. *The bottom line is: however long it takes, teach the group to trust you.*

# 3

## LEADERSHIP

Most managers are expected to have a *positive personal influence* on the job performance of the people who report directly to them. That's what *leadership* is.

But not all managers can do this. Unfortunately, *being required to lead* and actually *leading effectively* are two different things.

The actual leadership *performance* of managers covers a wide range:

- The *most effective* leaders ("good bosses") bring out the best in almost any group, under almost any circumstances.

- The *next best* leaders bring out the best in certain groups under certain circumstances.

- *Mediocre* leaders have little effect on their employees' job performances, one way or the other.

- *Demotivating* leaders ("bad bosses") actually make their subordinates less productive.

How common is each type kind of leader? There are no reliable figures. The number of good and bad bosses probably differs from one company to another. However, an educated guess or approximation would be that *on average*:

- 15 percent of all managers fit the definition of good bosses

- 30 percent fit the definition of next best leaders

- 50 percent are mediocre leaders

- 5 percent are bad bosses

Companies that have more good bosses and fewer mediocre or bad bosses have a major competitive advantage. Their employees get *more* work done and do it *better* at no greater *cost* than the employees of comparable companies. That translates into big gains in both productivity and profits.

## WHAT MAKES LEADERS EFFECTIVE?

Effective leaders provide whatever their subordinates *lack* to be fully effective themselves. That could be: confidence, information, recognition, discipline, or in some cases, nothing at all.

### DEVELOP YOUR EMPLOYEES

When employees don't feel equal to their task, you want to *build their self-confidence*. Show them *how* to succeed, *praise* their progress, and demonstrate your *confidence* in their abilities.

### COMMUNICATE CLEARLY

When employees have incomplete or incorrect information, you should *set them straight*. Give them facts that are up-to-date, reliable, and clear. Avoid complicated, evasive explanations.

### APPRECIATE YOUR EMPLOYEES' WORK

Effective leaders *never take work for granted*. When workers do what is expected of them—*especially* under difficult conditions—make sure they know that you are *aware* of it, and *appreciate* it.

### SET APPROPRIATE LIMITS

When workers don't take their responsibilities seriously, or try to evade established rules, make it clear that you *won't tolerate it.*

Note: Effective leaders don't hesitate to discipline employees when necessary, but only appropriately, in private, and after adequate warning. The goal of disciplinary action is not to humiliate, but to convince the employee that further misconduct would be a serious mistake.)

### DON'T INTERFERE

When employees are reliable, self-motivated, and self-disciplined, *don't impose unnecessary leadership* on them. Instead, remain ready to assist, but do not interfere unless they ask for help.

Effective leaders primarily concern themselves with satisfying the needs of the people they lead. The common elements in the examples above are the leader's ability to *diagnose* what subordinates need to be *effective* and *select an appropriate leadership style* to satisfy those needs. Above all, effective leaders must be adaptable: they must *fit their approach* to the people they are leading. Companies can greatly improve their performance by helping their managers become leaders (see Figure 4).

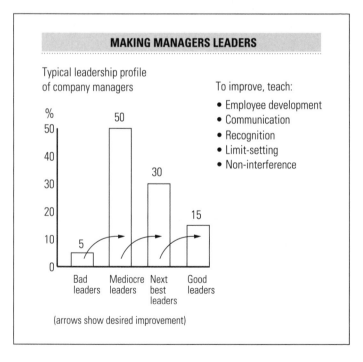

**Figure 4.**

## WHAT MAKES LEADERS INEFFECTIVE?

Ineffective leaders are primarily concerned with satisfying their own needs, rather than the needs of the people they are supposed to lead.

- Some managers become obsessed with constantly demonstrating that *they are the boss*. Their real purpose is to show everyone that they are tough. Their leadership style consists mainly of threats. They are nearly always bad bosses; that is, they make their people *less* productive.

- Some managers are *perfectionists* who demand improbably high performance standards from subordinates. They don't praise acceptable work if it isn't perfect, and they don't praise perfect work, because they don't want subordinates to become over-confident. They are so preoccupied with proving their own superiority that they are impossible to please. People with this unrealistic attitude tend to be mediocre leaders (at best).

- Some managers treat everyone they are supposed to lead in the same way, without regard to differing needs. For example, they may use a cheerleader approach, exhorting everyone to work harder. They may use a "hands-off" approach, hoping that everyone will motivate themselves. They cling to the method with which they feel comfortable, regardless of whether it works. These *one-size-fits-all* leaders are likely to be effective only some of the time, and ineffective most other times.

## ARE EFFECTIVE LEADERS BORN OR MADE?

Some leaders have an instinctive feel for the role. They seem to sense how to bring out the best in everyone they meet as if they were born to lead. But leaders with this gift are rare. There simply aren't enough of them to fill all the jobs that require leadership. So, as a practical matter, most leaders can use help to become better leaders.

## HOW CAN YOU BECOME A MORE EFFECTIVE LEADER?

Effective leadership is more like *coaching* than cheerleading. Study your subordinates. Get to know them. Listen to them. Try to build on their strengths. If they have any significant weaknesses, try to strengthen them, or better still, to make them unimportant.

Your objective is not to *remake* anyone, but to help your people to reach their own potential. Your role is to help them become the most effective version of *themselves* that they can attain.

# 4

# UNIONS

The National Labor Relations Act is one of the hard facts of life for every American company, *regardless* of whether it is currently unionized.

If your company is *not* unionized, the Act nevertheless:

- gives your workers the *right* to try to bring in a union, if they want to;

- requires your company to permit all employees to vote on whether to be represented by a union.

- If 30 percent of your employees request such an election and if a simple majority (50 percent +1) of the workers who vote favor a union, the Act requires your company to *negotiate* a contract with that union, and to be bound by the terms of that contract.

- If your company is already unionized, the Act requires your company to live with the terms of its union contract, even if they are costly and result in inefficiency.

Obviously, unions can create costly disadvantages for a company. That's why most nonunion companies are eager to stay that way.

## STRATEGIES FOR NONUNIONIZED COMPANIES

Most nonunionized companies adopt either a *proactive* or a *reactive* strategy toward the possibility that its workers may try to form a union.

• A company that uses a proactive strategy tries to minimize the risk that employees would call for an election in the first place. Without waiting for complaints, it seeks to eliminate even *potential* sources of employee discontent.

• A company that uses a reactive strategy does not become actively involved with employee complaints until an election has been called. It then seeks to win that election by arguing that workers would be better off *without* a union.

Each strategy has its advantages:

| **Proactive** | **Reactive** |
|---|---|
| • more likely to prevent unionization in the longs run. | • costs less, as long as workers show no interest in unions |
| • although costly, ultimately costs less than unionization.* | |

But each strategy also has its disadvantages:

| **Proactive** | **Reactive** |
|---|---|
| • can result in unnecessary concessions to workers. | • If employees call an election, the odds already favor the union.** |

## The Logic of Each Strategy

The *logic* of the proactive strategy is the same as an insurance policy: You pay now to avoid paying more later. The *logic* of the reactive strategy is the same as going without insurance: *maybe* you won't need it.

---

*The main disadvantages of unionization are the costs of inflexible work assignments, long strikes, and higher wage and benefit charges.*

**Consider the mathematics of union elections: The union already has the support of 30 percent of the employees. The contest is largely over the uncommitted 70 percent. To win, the union must gain or:ly two out of every seven uncommitted votes (not quite 29 percent). For management to win, it must gain five out of seven uncommitted votes (more than 70 percent). Even before the campaign begins, the odds favor the union by 7 to 3. Management could still win, but it would be an uphill battle.*

## The Tactics of Each Strategy

The *tactics* of the two strategies are also different:

| **Proactive** | **Reactive** |
|---|---|
| • actively seeks out sources of employee complaints and corrects them, or at least explains why they can't be corrected. | • assumes that worker complaints are exaggerated, or even invented, and therefore ignores them. |
| • in the absence of major complaints, seeks out minor ones to prevent them from turning into major complaints. | • in the absence of major complaints, "lets sleeping dogs lie." |
| • recognizes informal leaders among workers as spokespersons; respects and tries to influence their views. | • takes an adversarial attitude toward informal leaders among workers, regards them as trouble-makers, tries to get rid of them. |

Basically, unions argue that a conflict of interest between management and labor is inevitable. Therefore, (the argument goes) the "little guys" (labor) had better band together to effectively resist the "big guys" (management).

The most important single thing management can do to counter that argument is to avoid reinforcing it. Don't take an *adversarial* ("us against them") attitude toward workers.

## STRATEGY FOR UNIONIZED COMPANIES

Unionized companies must try to minimize the disadvantages of their labor contracts. This entails creating conditions that allow the local union's leadership to interpret the contract flexibly, and accommodate management on at least some matters.

Two strategies can be helpful. The first is the same as the proactive strategy for non-union companies: seek out and eliminate sources of discontent *before* they grow into major issues.

The second is the old political game of trading favors: "If you do this for me, I'll do that for you." In this game, the rules are to bargain hard before you make any promises; but *always* to keep the promises. In working with a union, your *credibility* is your most important asset.

# 5

## MONEY

Money is the most *unavoidable* motivator. It is also the most *overrated, inefficient, expensive* and *complicated* motivator. Nevertheless, when used realistically, it can be an effective motivator.

- Money is an *unavoidable* motivator, simply because we can't live without it. Most people earn their living by selling their labor for pay. That's why, in most cases, the only way to get work done is to pay for it.

- Money is an *overrated* motivator because it's easy to confuse the *necessity* of an income with the *effort* that goes into earning it. Those are two different issues. Of course, most people would like to receive more pay. But would they earn that extra pay by putting more time and effort into their work? In most cases, the answer is no.

  Extra money is always welcome, of course, if you don't have to earn it. But most people are already working as hard as they really want to, and extra effort does not come cheap. The price of extra effort is often prohibitive, if money is the *only* incentive.

- Money is an *inefficient* motivator. It takes a lot of money to get most people to work only a little bit harder, and then, only for a little while.

- Money is also an *expensive* motivator because wages, salaries, and benefits can't be deferred. If you can't meet the payroll, you're out of business. And employment costs, especially for benefits, just keep on rising.

• Money is a *complicated* motivator because its effects depend on several other factors. Here are three of the most important:

> ➤ *Who* are you trying to motivate? (Some people are more money-motivated than others.)

> ➤ *What* do you want them to do? (Money has two effects on almost everyone. All other effects of money vary with the person.)

> ➤ *How* much money is involved? (A large amount of money has a much different effect than a small amount. Too small an amount may have no effect at all.)

Let's take a closer look at those three "complications."

## WHO IS MONEY-MOTIVATED?

Four groups are likely to work harder to increase their incomes:

• *Yuppies* (young, upwardly mobile professionals) who have not yet achieved incomes that support the lifestyles they want. Any increase in income gets them there faster.

• *Climbers* (previously poor people on the verge of owning property, or having spare funds, for the first time). They are almost, but not quite, in the middle class. Any increase in income gets them there faster.

Note: Both yuppies and climbers are only *temporarily* money-motivated, because eventually their incomes reach the desired level. After that, while they still *want* more money, it would take *very* large increases to make them *work harder* for it.

• *Money-makers* (people who are money-motivated). For them, making money is an end in itself. It is their lifelong passion. They usually become rich.

Note: You are unlikely to have to motivate many money-makers yourself, because most of them are self-employed.

• *Achievers* (people for whom accomplishment is an end in itself). Money is only a secondary motivator for them. But they expect to be paid what they are worth, because they out-accomplish their peers.

Note: All four of these groups, taken together, add up to less than 50 percent of the work force. For a *majority* of the work force then, money is not the *primary motivator.* By itself, it won't produce *extra effort.*

## WHAT WILL PEOPLE DO FOR MONEY?

Money has two predictable effects on most people. (All other effects of money vary from person to person, depending on circumstances.)

• Money is a very effective recruiting tool. The initial pay offer largely determines where people will work.

This is money's *main* motivational effect. It largely determines the amount and quality of talent that a company can employ. But it does not determine how hard that talent will work, or how cooperative, creative, or productive it will be. All of those effects are determined mainly by *nonfinancial* motivators, such as leadership and types of jobs.

• Money's second motivational effect occurs when people feel that their pay is unfair. That happens if a company doesn't match their salary to what they feel they give the company (their qualifications, responsibilities, and job performance).

Think of this in terms of an old-fashioned balance scale (see Figure 5).

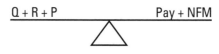

Q = Qualifications
R = Responsibilities
P = Job performance
NFM = Nonfinancial motivation

**Figure 5.**

If the value of what employees think they give to the employer is about equal to the value they think they receive, the scale is balanced, and the employees consider their pay to be more or less fair.

Note: Fairness has *no effect* on attitudes or job performance. They are determined mainly by the nonfinancial factors.

But consider what happens when employees feel underpaid (see Figure 6).

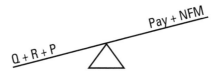

**Figure 6.**

A severe imbalance will motivate employees to restore the balance (see Figure 7). They can:

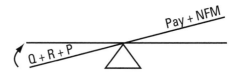

**Figure 7.**

- work harder to earn more pay (most won't do this, because it makes the imbalance worse).

- appeal to management for a pay increase (most won't do that either, because they consider it futile).

- leave the company (only the most highly qualified, or the most daring, are likely to risk that).

- restore the balance by *decreasing production* (by far the most common response).

Note: Pay can actually *demotivate* (cause a decrease in effort) if the employees consider it to be unfairly low.

## HOW MUCH MONEY MOTIVATES EXTRA EFFORT?

From a motivational standpoint, there are *two* kinds of pay. Each has different effects:

- *Fixed* pay (wages and salaries). This attracts people to companies and holds them there. However, pay that is too low can cause *turnover* and/or a *decrease* in production.

- *Variable* pay (commissions, bonuses, incentives, tips). These may increase effort, depending on the ratio of variable pay to fixed pay and the required standard of performance. If the ratio is high enough, and the standard is considered realistic, the result *could* be extra effort.

Note: The ratio between most salary increases and current salaries is not high enough to produce this effect. With variable pay, however, ratios of 20 percent or more are possible. It usually takes at least that much to make money into a real motivator.

## USING MONEY REALISTICALLY

As an inefficient motivator, money is usually too expensive for anything but attracting and holding talent and minimizing turnover and decreases in production.

But there are exceptions. Variable pay can stimulate extra effort when that effort can lead to major increases in production. But be prepared to spend liberally. Money motivation does *not* come cheap.

Fortunately, there are other incentives for hard work besides money. If your company's fixed pay is competitive, what it gets for its money is the opportunity to apply *nonfinancial* motivators. That is where managers get most of their real leverage on motivation. *Leadership* (already discussed) and *jobs* (discussed next) are the most important nonfinancial motivators.

# 6

## JOBS

Most jobs are designed for *efficiency*. The goal is to produce the most goods or services in the least time. This usually means designing jobs that are easily learned, narrowly specialized, and repetitive. Unfortunately, this makes many jobs *boring*.

### WHAT MAKES A JOB BORING?

The simplest way to make sure that a job can be easily learned is to hire people who are *overqualified* for it. They can *master* the job quickly. But after that, they *lose interest* in it just as quickly. Even people with limited abilities can be overqualified for a job that requires constant repetition of only a few simple steps.

Narrowly specialized, repetitive jobs offer very little *variety*. There is not much to hold the individual's *attention*. After a while, the employee does the work automatically, without much thought. This often causes such costly problems as *accidents, quality defects, absenteeism,* and *turnover*.

### WHAT MAKES A JOB MOTIVATING?

Here's an important point: No job is *inherently* boring. Whether a job holds (or loses) someone's attention depends on how well it matches that person's *abilities*:

- A job that *does not challenge* a person's abilities eventually becomes *boring*.

- A job that is *too difficult frustrates* the individual.

- A job that motivates someone demands all of the individual's abilities (and possibly more, so he or she is forced to *learn* in order to handle the job).

Note: It is much better to *avoid* the problem of boring work in the first place than to have to *fix* it afterward. In the long run, it is more efficient to design jobs to be *motivating*.

## Making Jobs Motivating

To understand how to design jobs that motivate people consider a typical *learning curve* and a typical *motivation curve:*

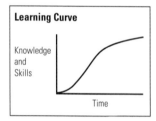

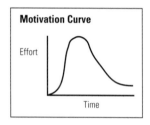

Both curves show how people change over time. The learning curve shows how much *knowledge* and *skill* people acquire as a function of *how long* they have been doing a job. The motivation curve shows how much *effort* people put into their work as a function of how long they have been doing it.

These curves indicate that both the *rate* of learning and the *strength* of motivation are at their maximum *early* in the process—that is, in the first year or two on the job. After that, people retain what they have learned, but both *new* learning and the effort put into work slow down.

The trick to making jobs motivating is to build a *new learning requirement* into them. This can be done in several ways, even when promotion is not practical.

- Add tasks that previously preceded (or followed) the job in question.

- Add tasks that were previously assigned to more skilled workers, or to professionals, or even to managers.

- Assign performance targets, then give workers freedom to pursue them as they deem fit.

Note: If a job changes sufficiently, a *pay increase* may be in order. The purpose of making jobs more motivating is not to get more work for the same pay, but to get *more valuable* work from more valuable (therefore, better-paid) employees.

## Changing Managers' Attitudes

To make workers more productive by making their jobs more motivating often requires a *change in managers' attitudes*. Giving employees the autonomy and means to challenge themselves and meet goals as they deem fit require managers to *turn over part of their functions* to their employees. But managers are still *accountable* for results, whether they control them or not.

Also, the functions that make workers' jobs more motivating also *motivate managers* (like making judgment calls).

Therefore, to make workers' jobs more motivating, managers have to *take risks* and *make sacrifices*. That calls for a high degree of *professionalism*.

*A final note of caution:* The strategy of cutting costs by making jobs more motivating works with many employees, *but not with all*. Some lack the *self-confidence* to feel comfortable with responsibility for their own decisions.

There is no reliable way to tell, in advance, how someone will react to a more demanding job. The best way to find out if this method works with individual workers is to experiment. Give them a job with a built-in learning requirement, and see what happens.

The risks of trying to make jobs more motivating are usually worth taking. The odds are favorable, but no experiment is a sure thing. Of course, the reason we need managers in the first place is that there are very few "sure things" in life, anyway.

# 7

## STRESS

Competition, deadlines, and constant pressure combine to make *stress* a tiresome fact of life in business. On the other hand, *too little* stress causes *complacency* and *inefficiency*. The trick is to *manage* stress so that it is always a stimulant but never a strain.

### EXCESS STRESS

Too much stress leads to *burnout, ethics violations,* and *substance abuse.*

- *Burnout* is a loss of energy, interest, and ambition, due to more prolonged stress than the individual can tolerate. Job performance suffers, sometimes drastically. A respite of some kind is necessary. Sometimes a transfer is the only solution.

- *Ethics violations* (taking bribes, falsifying records, etc.) are usually committed by people with previously clean records who ran into more temptation or pressure than they could handle.

    ➤ *Prevention* is better than punishment. But simply spelling out the rules or warning would-be violators is not enough. It is better not to put anyone's ethics under too much stress than to find out, too late, that they couldn't resist it.

    ➤ To "keep employees honest," managers should neither *tempt* them with the prospect of easy, but ill-gotten, gains, nor *threaten* them with punishments they would do anything to avoid. Pressure for performance should be in the "low to moderate" range. The only exception would be a genuine *emergency*.

• *Substance abuse* (alcohol, drugs) can be a misguided attempt to escape unpleasant emotions (loneliness, anxiety, low self-esteem). On-the-job substance abuse leads to *accidents, absenteeism,* and *below-standard job performance*.

> ➤ This problem has multiple causes, and job stress is only one of them. Therefore, reducing excessive job stress addresses only part of the problem—but an important part.

> ➤ Substance abuse requires *forceful intervention* by managers. Employees suspected of this problem should be required to seek professional help. Failure to insist on this only worsens the problem, and eventually makes it unmanageable.

## TOO LITTLE STRESS

When job performance has no particular *consequences* on income or job security, the most likely result is *sloppy work habits*. There may be a few exceptions: some employees maintain high standards due to *personal* pride. Others find satisfaction in the *work itself*. Otherwise, a lack of *pressure to perform* seems to make most people complacent.

Here are some symptoms to watch for:

• Indifference to *customer needs*

• More concern with doing work *easily* and *conveniently* than with doing it *effectively*

• Using work time for *non-work-related* activities,

• A tendency to use maximum number of allowable "*sick days.*"

The most *serious* effect is the tendency of any of these to *worsen,* or to spread from person to person. This indicates a growing belief by workers that management *accepts* such habits, or *doesn't care*.

The most dramatic demonstration of the effects of complacency can be seen in former *communist countries*. Workers were guaranteed a low, but secure, income in exchange for low levels of effort. This is one reason why the communist economies eventually collapsed.

## MANAGING STRESS

The strategy for *managing stress* is to avoid both extremes. We can't tolerate complacency, but neither can we risk aggravating the problems of burnout, ethical violations, or substance abuse.

The trick to avoiding the extremes of stress is to *monitor* the effects of your company's policies. Don't confuse the *intentions* of those policies with their *effects*. Many motivational problems turn out to be the *unintended side-effects* of well-intentioned management policies.

The easiest way to monitor the effects of stress is to keep accurate records of *absenteeism, lateness, turnover, transfer requests,* and in the case of unionized companies, *grievances* (formal complaints). An increase in any of these that exceeds normal variations is worth investigating.

A more sensitive way to monitor the effects of stress is with *employee attitude surveys*. These usually involve questionnaires, and are given *annually*. The strategy is to identify and defuse potential sources of stress *before* they can become excessive.

# 8

## MOTIVATING YOURSELF

Managers are responsible for motivating the employees who report to them. But who is responsible for motivating managers?

In an ideal world, each manager's immediate superior would have that responsibility. In the real world, managers are expected to motivate *themselves*.

*Self-motivation* is a deliberate, conscious effort to *control your emotions, stay focused* on what matters most, and give yourself *good advice*.

- Emotional control means *not over-reacting* to provocations, pressures, or other people's foolishness. Your attitude should be that it's your *job* to deal with these things, and you're going to deal with them *professionally*.

Note: An agitated manager gets everyone else agitated. If you're upset, try to avoid saying things you may regret later. *Remember:* you are the *master* of every thought you decided *not* to express, but you are the *slave* of everything you say aloud.

- Staying focused means always knowing your *priorities*. Begin each day by thinking through what needs to be accomplished. Prioritize those goals and memorize the first four or five. No matter what unexpected distractions may arise, those are the things you are going to get done, *come hell or high water*.

A focused manager helps everyone else to stay focused, *especially* when they are under pressure. The two things that matter most are your *example* and your *accessibility*. Make sure everyone knows that work pressure, like bad weather, is just another problem to handle and not a reason to lose sight of goals. Spend extra time *mingling* with your people when they're under pressure. Give them plenty of opportunities to speak to you, and to see at first hand that you intend to reach those goals.

- Giving yourself good advice means learning to provide for yourself what your own superiors may not provide. This includes *recognition, encouragement,* and an *incentive* to keep going under adverse conditions.

  ➤ It's always helpful when someone else is aware of, and appreciates, your good work. But when no one else has the sense to give you the recognition you deserve, give it to yourself. Treat yourself to something you like—even something simple, like a book you've been meaning to buy. Just shrug off the insensitivity of your superiors. They probably take you for granted because they know your work is good.

Note: *Never* make that mistake with *your* subordinates. Good work is too precious to be ignored. And recognition is the best guarantee that good work won't deteriorate into bad work.

  ➤ The stiffest test of anyone's motivation is to keep pursuing a goal under adverse conditions, especially when no one is offering encouragement. You have to decide whether the goal is *worth failing for*—that is, whether your goal is so important that the effort to reach it would be worthwhile, even if the odds are against success. If you feel that strongly about it, go for it.

Note: Mere persistence is no guarantee of success. But a lack of persistence guarantees failure. The key to *sensible persistence* is to choose your goals carefully. A goal worth committing yourself to is one you'd be proud to say you had tried your best to reach, regardless of whether you had ever actually attained it

## FOR FURTHER READING

My 1992 book, *Motivation in the Real World* (New York: Dutton), provides a more detailed coverage of the subjects discussed in this monograph.

A number of academic books provide a more scholarly treatment of the same subject. The best I have seen is John B. Winer's *Theories of Organizational Behavior* (Hinsdale, Ill.: Dryden, 1980). In my opinion, none of the more recent books of this type can match it for depth and scope. Nor is it really out of date, since its topics are still very relevant.

## ABOUT THE AUTHOR

Saul W. Gellerman is a management consultant, specializing in executive development and organization studies. He is the author of nine books, including *Motivation and Productivity* and *Motivation in the Real World.* He was formerly dean of the Graduate School of Management at the University of Dallas. Dr. Gellerman is based in Irving, Texas.

# The Management Master Series

The *Management Master Series* offers business managers leading-edge information on the best contemporary management practices. Written by highly respected authorities, each short "briefcase book" addresses a specific topic in a concise, to-the-point presentation, using both text and illustrations. These are ideal books for busy managers who want to get the whole message quickly.

Set 1 — Great Management Ideas:

1. *Management Alert: Don't Reform—Transform!*
   Michael J. Kami

2. *Vision, Mission, Total Quality: Leadership Tools for Turbulent Times*
   William F. Christopher

3. *The Power of Strategic Partnering*
   Eberhard E. Scheuing

4. *New Performance Measures*
   Brian H. Maskell

5. *Motivating Superior Performance*
   Saul W. Gellerman

6. *Doing and Rewarding: Inside a High-Performance Organization*
   Carl G. Thor

Future sets will cover such topics as Total Quality, Customer Service, Leadership, and Innovation. For complete details, call 800-394-6868 or fax 800-394-6286.

**SPECIAL OFFER:** Individual books are priced at $15.95. Buy all six books in Set 1 and save 10%! Order item code MMS-1 to get the discount. (Prices are subject to change.)

PRODUCTIVITY PRESS, Dept. BK, PO Box 13390, Portland, OR 97213-0390
Phone (503) 235-0600                                    Fax (503) 235-0909

## BOOKS FROM PRODUCTIVITY PRESS

Productivity Press publishes and distributes materials on continuous improvement in productivity, quality, and the creative involvement of all employees. Many of our products are direct source materials from Japan that have been translated into English for the first time and are available exclusively from Productivity. Supplemental products and services include membership groups, conferences, seminars, in-house training and consulting, audio-visual training programs, and industrial study missions. Call toll-free 1-800-394-6868 for our free catalog.

### Handbook for Productivity Measurement and Improvement
*William F. Christopher and Carl G. Thor, eds.*
An unparalleled resource! In over 100 chapters, nearly 80 front-runners in the quality movement reveal the evolving theory and specific practices of world-class organizations. Spanning a wide variety of industries and business sectors, they discuss quality and productivity in manufacturing, service industries, profit centers, administration, nonprofit and government institutions, health care and education. Contributors include Robert C. Camp, Peter F. Drucker, Jay W. Forrester, Joseph M. Juran, Robert S. Kaplan, John W. Kendrick, Yasuhiro Monden, and Lester C. Thurow. Comprehensive in scope and organized for easy reference, this compendium belongs in every company and academic institution concerned with business and industrial viability.
ISBN 1-56327-007-2 / 1344 pages / $90.00 / Order HPM-B237

### Fast Focus on TQM
#### A Concise Guide to Companywide Learning
*Derm Barrett*
Finally, here's one source for all your TQM questions. Compiled in this concise, easy-to-read handbook are definitions and detailed explanations of over 160 key terms used in TQM. Organized in a simple alphabetical glossary form, the book can be used either as a primer for anyone being introduced to TQM or as a complete reference guide. It helps to align teams, departments, or entire organizations in a common understanding and use of TQM terminology. For anyone entering or currently involved in TQM, this is one resource you must have.
ISBN 1-56327-049-8 / 186 pages / $19.95 / Order FAST-B237

PRODUCTIVITY PRESS, Dept. BK, PO Box 13390, Portland, OR 97213-0390
Phone (503) 235-0600                                     Fax (503) 235-0909

**Feedback Toolkit**
**16 Tools for Better Communication in the Workplace**
*Rick Maurer*
In this follow-up to his successful book *Caught in the Middle,* Rick Maurer explores the issue of feedback by both employer and employee. Feedback keeps the lines of communication open and serves as a major motivational tool, yet many managers do not give feedback to their employees or give it the wrong way. Maurer offers sixteen specific tools any manager can follow when giving feedback. Written in a fun, easy-to-read style, this concise book can be read quickly but should be absorbed slowly and followed carefully. Managing employees must be done correctly to bring out people's maximum potential. Everyone wants to know how they're doing. They prefer to hear only the good, but they know they must hear the bad. In *Feedback Toolkit*, you'll learn how to dish out the good and the bad, while getting the results you want.
ISBN 1-56327-056-0 /109 pages / $15.00 / Order FEED-B237


**Individual Motivation**
**Removing the Blocks to Creative Involvement**
*Etienne Minarik*
The key to gaining the competitive advantage in a saturated market is to use existing resources more efficiently and creatively. This book shows managers how to turn employees' "negative individualism" into creativity and initiative. It describes the shift in corporate culture necessary to enable front-line employees to use their knowledge about product and process to the company's greatest benefit.
ISBN 0-915299-85-2 / 263 pages / $29.95 / Order INDM-B237

PRODUCTIVITY PRESS, Dept. BK, PO Box 13390, Portland, OR 97213-0390
Phone (503) 235-0600                                    Fax (503) 235-0909

TO ORDER: Write, phone, or fax Productivity Press, Dept. BK, P.O. Box 13390, Portland, OR 97213-0390, phone 1-800-394-6868, fax 1-800-394-6286. Send check or charge to your credit card (American Express, Visa, MasterCard accepted).

U.S. ORDERS: Add $5 shipping for first book, $2 each additional for UPS surface delivery. Add $5 for each AV program containing 1 or 2 tapes; add $12 for each AV program containing 3 or more tapes. We offer attractive quantity discounts for bulk purchases of individual titles; call for more information.

INTERNATIONAL ORDERS: Write, phone, or fax for quote and indicate shipping method desired. For international callers, telephone number is 503-235-0600 and fax number is 503-235-0909. Prepayment in U.S. dollars must accompany your order (checks must be drawn on U.S. banks). When quote is returned with payment, your order will be shipped promptly by the method requested.

NOTE: Prices are in U.S. dollars and are subject to change without notice.

NOTES